Publisher's Cataloging-in-Publication
(Provided by Quality Books, Inc.)

Hall, Kaye, 1937-
    Stop and stay put : a guide to safer adventures
outdoors / by Kaye Hall.
    p. cm.
    SUMMARY: Two children embark on a camping
adventure and, with the help of a heroic search dog
and the acronym SAFER, learn basic wilderness skills.

    Audience: Grades Preschool through 5.
    LCCN 2010905715
    ISBN-13: 9780982675601
    ISBN-10: 0982675607

    1. Outdoor life--Safety measures--Juvenile fiction.
[1. Outdoor life--Fiction. 2. Safety--Fiction.] I. Title.

PZ7.H1452Sto 2010   [E]
                          QBI10-600124

DEDICATION

This book is dedicated to my dog, Julot, and all of his four footed search buddies who do so much to save lives. ~ Kaye Hall

GOOD CHOICES
NATIONAL PARK
ENTRANCE

STOP AND STAY PUT

A Guide to Safer Adventures Outdoors

When they spotted the park entrance Colin and Katy began squirming in their seatbelts. This was Colin's first camping adventure ever. He would be here a whole week. Tired from the long car trip, he was eager to run in the woods.

They drove past a group riding donkeys. Both exclaimed, "Oh, wow!" at the same time.

Mom and Dad put up the tent and set out their gear. Katy and Colin helped a little between playing and chasing each other. Dad put their food in a bear proof box and hung it on a tree branch. "Remember, no food in the tent or left lying around," he warned.

"Yes," laughed Katy. "Remember the three bears in the story about Goldilocks. We don't want bears in our tent."

Dad set out for Logan Creek with fishing gear. Colin wanted to go with him, but his parents said he must first attend a talk about Safety in the Park. So here he was with his mom and sister. At least the group included other children his age and he'd soon have new friends.

A man in a crisp uniform with an orange bandana tipped his hat and welcomed them with open arms. "Hola, I'm your teacher today—Roberto Gonzales at your service. Call me Ranger Rob." His mustache twitched as he greeted everyone with a big smile.

He gave each of them a map of the park. "Stay on the trails," he advised. "Trails protect the wildlife and also help keep people from getting lost.

Now let's talk about how to keep from getting lost. And talk about what to do if you get lost—in spite all your best efforts."

Ranger Rob brought out a chart with large letters S.A.F.E.R. printed. "I want all of you to know what these letters stand for," he said.

"**S** is for ***STOP*** **and** ***STAY PUT*** when lost so we can find you. And when you stop, where's the best place to stay put?" he asked them.

A girl answered, "Where it is cool and shady."

"Today, yes. Other days may be cold or rainy. Then keeping warm and dry is very important. Use a tree, rocks, or something you have with you for shelter from the sun or from the cold.

"You also want to do all you can to be visible—so you can be seen by searchers. Pilots fly overhead. You can make big signs on the ground.   Use branches, rocks or draw in the dirt. Pick an open area close to where you'll be. Bright colors and shiny objects are helpful."

He held up a mirror and showed everyone how to flash signals from sunlight with it. "At night you can use a flashlight."

"If it starts raining, there might be lightning," said Mom.

"Great point," answered Ranger Rob. "If it does start to rain, stay away from the tallest trees and the tops of hills."

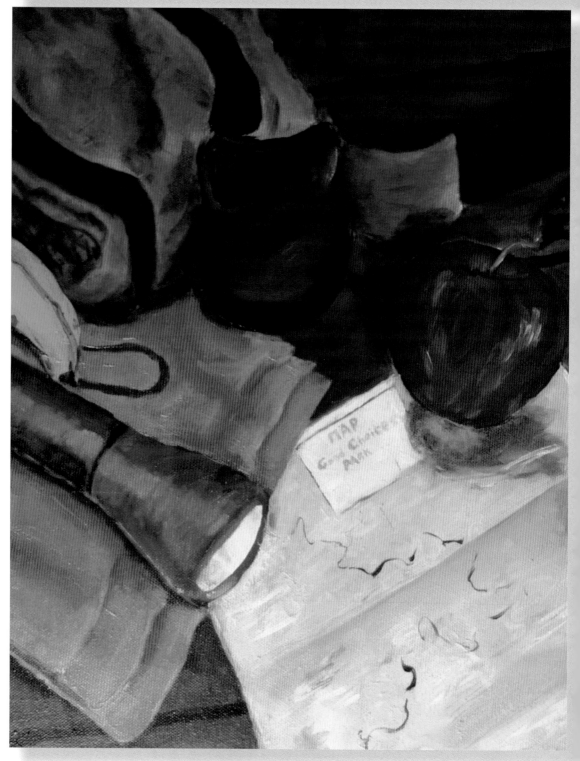

"Now **A** stands for **ADULT**—Tell an adult—a grown-up—where you are going," Ranger Rob continued. "That gives searchers a place to start looking."

"The next letter is **F**—Go with a **FRIEND**. Why is it important not to go alone?"

Several answers came at once. "Two heads are better than one;" "If you get hurt, your friend is there to help;" "Two or more would make it easier to scare off a bear."

"**E**, of course, is for your **EQUIPMENT KIT** which you *always* take with you," Ranger Rob said. "Don't leave your tent without it." He gave each of the children an orange plastic trash bag and a whistle to add to their equipment kit. "Blow this whistle in an emergency," he said. "It's not for fun, but to be used when you really need someone's help."

"What is the trash bag for?" one boy asked.

"You can fill it with leaves to make a mat to sit on," answered Ranger Rob. "Or you can carry things like water or food in it. If it's hot you can prop it up for shade. But let me show you how to wear it to keep dry and warm." He poked a hole close to the bottom of the bag just big enough to fit over the boy's head. It covered him like a poncho.

"Now this is important." Ranger Rob's voice deepened. He stopped smiling and made eye contact with each and every person. "Plastic bags are dangerous if there's not a big enough hole to get plenty of air. And you must keep them away from little children for that reason."

All were eager to have food and drink in their equipment kit. Colin had some nuts, juice and an apple. The girl next to him had water and a banana.

You can live a long time without food and water," said Ranger Rob. "But you are more likely to get hurt or make mistakes if you are hungry or thirsty."

"And the same can be said for the next letter—**R** for **REST** often. You'll be a lot safer if you are not tired."

"Wow!" he lifted his hat and then put it back on his head. "That's what S.A.F.E.R. stands for. Can you remember all that?" Then, to their surprise, he pulled out a guitar and sang this song:

 # THE SAFER SONG

Come along with me

We're gonna go outdoors

Where you can see some things

You never saw before

Where the trees are tall,

And the breezes blow

And you can feel so free

Just make sure you know

You can be:

SAFER

CHORUS

SAFER - S for STOP AND STAY PUT

SAFER - A for TELL AN ADULT

SAFER - F for GO WITH A FRIEND

SAFER - E for TAKE YOUR EQUIPMENT KIT

SAFER—R for MAKE SURE YOU REST

S. A. F. E. R.

If you listen you'll see

That's what you'll be

(Repeat the Chorus)

After the talk, Mom wanted to purchase some postcards and a bulb for Colin's flashlight. "Can we walk back on our own instead of waiting with you?" begged Colin.

"If you promise to stay together, you may," Mom agreed. "And if you stay on the Brennen Trail. It goes directly back to our camp. I'll follow in a few minutes."

Colin and Katy trotted along the trail toward their tent, exploring every rock and flower. "I'm eight; I'm not going to get lost," Colin boasted.

Katy shook her head and rolled her eyes.

Suddenly a swallowtail butterfly flew by. Colin's latest hobby was studying butterflies. He ran off the trail to follow it into the trees.

"Colin," yelled Katy. "We promised to stay on the trail and go right to our tent."

But Colin was too excited to hear.   He kept running after it and vanished into the bushes.

The butterfly landed on a bush by a small stream. Beside the stream on a large flat rock, Colin found a large bullfrog. He bent over and said, "Hello, frog."

The fat green bullfrog croaked a husky, "SAAAFERRR."

Colin stood up, shrugged and stepped over the stream. His boots left deep footprints beside the stream, but Colin did not notice.

In a tree just beyond the stream, he heard a bird singing a song. It sounded a like the robin in his backyard. But he spotted its red head and its bright yellow breast. It was definitely not a robin.

"I know my whistle is just for emergencies, but I wonder if it could make me sound like a bird," Colin thought. He came close to the bird, stopped, and pulled out his whistle.

His sudden movements scared the bird. It flew away right over his head. Colin quickly started to put his whistle away, but it fell to the ground.

Colin did not notice because he spied two spotted fawns dashing away with their mother, waving their white tails. He followed them excitedly and forgot the whistle.

Colin soon lost sight of the deer. He decided to go back to his campsite. He looked around, but he could not see the trail.

He was afraid, and guessed the trail was beyond some bushes. When he reached the bushes, the area did not look familiar. Growing around some of the bushes was a plant Ranger Rob had warned them to avoid—poison oak!

Colin wandered from tree to tree. His stomach growled. His feet were tired, and he was very much alone. He thought of the term S.A.F.E.R. and wished he had a friend or an adult with him.

He heard a very fast drum, drum, drumming noise and went to investigate. He found a woodpecker pecking on an old log. "Which way is the trail?" he asked.

But the woodpecker ignored him. It stopped drumming and sang "YA KIT! YA KIT! YA KIT!" as it flew up to a hole in a tree to feed its babies.

"My kit? Oh, yes. I have food in my kit," he remembered. He pulled out the nuts and ate them as he walked along. Then he drank the juice.

He tried to remember what Ranger Rob had told them. "S.A.F.E.R. What did the S stand for?"

"Well, this is an emergency"; he decided and reached for his whistle. It was not in his kit. Colin yelled for help. But without his whistle, the sound did not carry. His voice tired quickly. And the sun was getting lower in the sky. He was afraid.

He came to a hill full of holes. He was tired and did not want to climb the hill. Chipmunks were running in and out of the holes. They chattered at each other. Their chatter sounded like a hint to him, "Sssss."

Colin kept thinking about S, but he couldn't remember what it meant. Suddenly one of the chipmunks stopped running around. It looked at Colin, not moving a muscle. It stayed very, very still. Several minutes passed. It still did not move. It just stayed put.

"That's it!" Colin finally remembered, "STOP and STAY PUT is what the S in 'S.A.F.E.R.' stands for." And so he stopped and looked for a good place to stay put.

"I must be visible," he thought, "I must be out in the open. I'll use that tree and those bushes to protect me from the wind. I can still be seen from there."

But the ground was damp and hard. He pulled the orange trash bag out of his equipment kit. Colin filled it with leaves and dumped several loads into a thick pile. Then he sat down.

A breeze made him shiver. He remembered how Ranger Rob had showed him to make the bag into a poncho. He poked a hole in the bottom of the bag for his face and pulled it over his head. Colin put the bag on and soon felt much warmer. "And I'm much easier to see all covered with an orange bag," he thought.

Meanwhile, when Colin did not come back, Katy ran as fast as she could down the trail. She ran straight into her mom's arms.

She told her mom that Colin had gone off the trail and into the woods. Mom blew on Katy's whistle and called for him. But Colin did not answer. So they went to tell Ranger Rob.

"Don't worry," Ranger Rob said as he put his hat back on. "You came to me right away. That is very good. Even if Colin forgets to STOP and STAY PUT, he won't have gone very far.

"Ranger Ryan," he called. "Call out our search team. Send a searcher to locate Colin's dad on the Logan Trail. Send someone to the campgrounds in case Colin gets back there on his own. I won't wait for you to get the team ready. I'll start searching now with SAR Shannon and Seeker."

Katy wondered who SAR Shannon and Seeker were. Ranger Rob led them to a cabin with a sign that said, "SEARCH AND RESCUE." He knocked on the door and a woman answered. A black dog with a long furry coat sat beside her. The woman was wearing an orange uniform shirt with the letters S.A.R. above her pocket.

"This is Shannon and her trailing dog, Seeker," introduced Ranger Rob.

Seeker was friendly and even shook hands with Katy.

Ranger Rob explained to Shannon that Colin was missing. Shannon put a harness and an orange vest marked "SEARCH DOG" on Seeker, and put a pack on her own back.

"First," she said, "I need something of Colin's that no one else has touched lately."

They rushed back to the family tent where Mom found Colin's hairbrush in his bag. Shannon had Seeker sniff the hairbrush so he would know Colin's unique smell.

Then Shannon commanded Seeker, "Find him!" Seeker walked ahead of them back along the path with his nose close to the ground.

All of a sudden he left the path into the woods right where Colin had run after the swallowtail butterfly. Shannon followed him. She held onto Seeker's long line so she could keep him in sight.

At the small stream, Seeker looked at the bullfrog. "SAAAFERRR," it croaked again and leapt away.

Seeker wagged his tail and paused at some footprints. "Look!" exclaimed Mom. "Those look like prints from Colin's boots!"

Under a tree, Seeker stopped and sat down. Between his paws was a small orange object. "A whistle!" exclaimed Shannon. "Is this Colin's?"

Seeker wagged his tail, "*Yes*."

"Well done, Seeker," praised Shannon. "Let's go on." Seeker gave a shake to clear his nose. Then again he picked up Colin's scent.

Ranger Rob radioed where the whistle had been found to Ranger Ryan. Then Ranger Ryan knew to move his search team farther south from their start point. Seeker continued his trailing.

The deer watched from their hiding place in the bushes where they had bedded down for the night.

"I do wish Colin would STOP and STAY PUT," sighed Shannon. "Did you teach him to do that, Ranger Rob?"

"Yes, I taught him S.A.F.E.R." answered Ranger Rob with a worried frown. "But maybe he forgot STOP and STAY PUT. He also forgot to go with a FRIEND. He forgot to tell an ADULT where he was going. And now we know he has lost his whistle."

"And he didn't go straight up the trail to our camp with Katy as he promised," added Mom.

Seeker followed a scent path which seemed to zigzag around in a huge circle. He passed a dead tree where a woodpecker was too busy pecking away to notice them.

Katy worried about her brother.

Now it was getting dark, so they turned on their flashlights and headlamps.

Suddenly a great horned owl called, "Who, who, who," from a tree limb.

"Colin," answered Katy, pointing her finger at the owl. "We're looking for Colin, that's who."

But the owl flew off and kept repeating, "Who, who, who," as he flew away.

They passed a hill checkered with little holes. "Snakes?" asked Katy moving closer to her mom.

"Chipmunks," said Ranger Rob, "but they have all gone to bed and are fast asleep by now."

Suddenly Seeker surged forward toward a pile of orange plastic. It was Colin! Seeker covered his face with kisses while Colin hugged the furry dog. He had been found!

"Good job, Seeker!" everyone exclaimed.

They all stood around Colin, laughing in relief. Moments later Ranger Ryan's team arrived. Colin got a big hug from his dad.

Later as they returned to the campsite, Colin walked beside his new furry friend. He remarked, "I'll never again forget what S.A.F.E.R. stands for."

Ranger Ryan's team cheered at Colin's resolve. They began singing 'The S.A.F.E.R. Song.' Colin laughed and joined in as they all walked together down the trail.

THE END

THINGS TO REMEMBER

1. If you don't know where you are, what should you do?

2. What does SAFER stand for?

3. Why stay on trails?

4. Why was it important for Dad to tell his family he would be on Logan Creek?

5. Why are rest, food and drink important?

6. What things should you keep in mind in choosing a place to STOP and STAY PUT?

7. What could you do if there was rain and lightening?

THINGS TO REMEMBER

8. Colin made a lot of mistakes, but what did he do right?

9. How do you know if it's safe to talk to the strangers searching for you when you're lost?

10. What is a whistle for?

11. How can you use a trash bag?

12. How can you make yourself more visible if you are lost?

13. How soon should you tell an officer like Ranger Rob that someone might be lost? Why?

ABOUT THE AUTHOR

Kaye Hall is a trailing handler for the Napa County Sheriff's Volunteer Search and Rescue Team and the California Rescue Dog Association. In the county and elsewhere in the state, she is called to search for missing persons with her dog. She is also a tracking judge for the American Kennel Club (where dogs follow the scent of a person as a sport.) This sport is great fun for the dogs and their handlers, and it inspires many to continue with search and rescue activities. In Kaye's spare time she is an artist and her paintings illustrate this book.

"During my years as a trailing canine handler, I have participated in many searches for missing persons including preschoolers and octogenarians. I have presented countless demonstrations about outdoor safety to school children.

These experiences have convinced me that good materials are needed to support the success of search and rescue missions, and ultimately will reduce the necessity of searches."

ABOUT THE DOG

Julot is a Belgian Sheepdog with the most prestigious American Kennel Club performance rating, Champion Tracker. Julot certified as a mission-ready trailing dog shortly before his second birthday. Trailing means he can follow where a person has gone by their unique scent.

He has trained with Kaye and her search canine unit since he was ten weeks old. He has "found" over 150 different people during his training exercises which included following persons who were in cars, who went up streams that require swimming as well as scenting, in wilderness and urban areas, on trails both fresh and up to six days old. Julot has been deployed with Kaye to search for missing persons since his certification. His efforts have often been beneficial for searches.

He has a fan club of many law enforcement officers. He also loves to dance. He loves the attention in parades and demonstrations. Once strapped into a helicopter, he loves flying and peering out the open door.

THANK YOU

A special thanks to the faculty in the Art Department of Napa Valley College, especially Fain Hancock and Nancy Willis for their guidance, assistance and helpful critiques.

Kudos to the members of the Napa writers group of the Society of Children's Book Writers and Illustrators for their help and encouragement.

Carolynne Gamble with her "eagle eye" has edited, designed and "tightened up" the book's flow.

Christie Farrell photographed my 18" X 24" oil paintings. Jim Horton photographed me and Julot.

The *SAFER Song* on the CD is by Rita Abrams with Kaye Hall. The children who accompanied the vocalist, Mike Shapiro, are Juan Cerda, Sebastian Gonzalez, Jayson Solais, and Ryan Lee Nelson. A *Word from the Animals* is narrated by Rita Abrams and the animals. The CD was produced and engineered at Beatrecords, San Francisco, California.   - *Kaye Hall*

SEARCH AND RESCUE

SAR

WWW.SEARCH-DOG-HEROES.COM

And a very special thanks to my mission ready trailing dog, Julot. He and my teammates in CARDA and the Napa County Sheriff's Volunteer Search and Rescue Group have taught me much about search and rescue.

Visit the website for the latest Search Dog Heroes at www.search-dog-heroes.com.

THE SAFER SONG

Come along with me
We're gonna go outdoors
Where you can see some things
You never saw before
Where the trees are tall,
And the breezes blow
And you can feel so free
Just make sure you know
You can be:

CHORUS

SAFER - S for STOP AND STAY PUT

SAFER - A for TELL AN ADULT

SAFER - F for GO WITH A FRIEND

SAFER - E for TAKE YOUR EQUIPMENT KIT

SAFER—R for MAKE SURE YOU REST

S. A. F. E. R.

If you listen you'll see
That's what you'll be
(Repeat the Chorus)